The writers' group.

Left to right back: Christina Hale (far left) and Janet Slack (far right)

Left to right middle - Marie Hunt, Kathy Hardill, Shirley Ellis.

Acknowledgements

We would like to express our sincere gratitude to Derick Ferguson, Secretary Age Concern Carlton & District for his ceaseless encouragement in collecting the stories for this book; to the members of 'The Mayfield' at Age Concern Carlton who have provided us with copious recollections of their lives; to their families who have helped fill in gaps of family history; also, to the staff of The Mayfield Centre who have helped facilitate the meetings where we collected the stories. We would also like to thank Piotr Grzybowski for helping to proof read the stories with his eagle eye. Last, but my no means, least, thanks to the "ghost writers" of The Age Concern Carlton Creative Writing Group who kept writing even during the Covid-19 lockdown of 2020 and 2021!

Contents

Introduction

There are two groups of stars in this project – the members of The Mayfield Centre at Age Concern and The Age Concern Carlton Writers' Group.

This project emerged from our every-day interaction with the people who enjoy the activities our centre offers, and often, in the normal course of events we find ourselves sharing many stories. The common perception is it's only young people who write adventure stories, but in our group, we regularly reflect on the many and varied adventures of life, and so a project was born, resulting in us capturing the life-stories of people with whom we interact on a regular basis.

The ages of these people range, in the main, from late 60's to those who are in their 90's. Their backgrounds are varied, as are the countries they come from, England, Ireland, Scotland, Italy and Iraq. The stories extend from growing up in war-torn Britain, to escaping the poverty of rural Italy, to fleeing the persecutions experienced by Kurds in Iraq.

We are often guilty of neglecting to write things down about our lives while there is time. But the importance of preserving our history is clear. Our storytellers have been so keen to recount their tales and some have written their own stories, even poems. Many families have become engaged in sifting out photos and adding to what their relatives at The Mayfield Centre have told us. Families have been aware that grandad's or grandma's tale is worth recording. During the project, some have suffered illnesses and a few died, making the garnering of these unique tales all the more vital.

We have called this book **A Second Voice**. The reason for this is that the first **Voice** was an anthology of the stories and histories of Carlton & District Age Concern Writers' Group. This book, however, goes a step beyond that, as those same women who produced the stories and poems for Voice have now become the **voice** for members of the (Age Concern) Mayfield Centre. The Writers' group have spent enthralling hours, talking to those who wanted to share their stories, asking questions, writing notes, and essentially, they have become their ghost writers, (though we mention their names in tribute to their efforts) capturing recollections of times past. We have also tasked the writing group to try their hand at writing poetry. These poems we have called "Fragments" as they are fragments of the histories, small pieces which shine a light on aspects of the main story.

Collecting the stories and writing them has resulted in a roller-coaster of emotions: humbling, tearful, at times shocking, impressive, inspiring and therapeutic, both for those imparting their tales and those collecting them. It has been a privilege to be the collectors as the people freely shared very personal, and at times, poignant memoirs. We realise that people were giving a huge part of themselves in sharing such intimate and emotional details.

It has also been rewarding to see how the writers have progressed from writing their own stories, to becoming ghost writers. As a group, we have kept going throughout the Covid Pandemic which started in March 2020. This has not been easy as the impetus and inspiration normally found in the writers' group has hardly been present. We have had to phone and email each other, and some people have hand-written ideas and posted them for editing. When we could, we met at one member's house, (always sticking to the guidelines!) and enjoyed the luxury of being human: speaking, joking, but also editing, enhancing and writing more. We don't think the writers will mind us saying, but their average age is 82 and they all tell us they are still learning about writing.

There has been a huge engagement in this project. Stories of life, the human condition, stories folk may have told their children or grandchildren are preserved in this most worthwhile book. Some people have spoken for themselves but for those who couldn't, we have given them a second voice.

Derick Ferguson, Secretary Age Concern
and Janet Slack, Project Co-ordinator/Editor

Pat

After a wonderful wedding day,
For which friends and family paved the way,
Grand promises of a lovely life,
Free from any trouble and strife.
But all too soon I became aware
My husband had heavy alcohol problems to bear.

Nine years on, with a lovely daughter,
Australia beckoned and we felt we oughta
Follow our dream for a new way of living,
One that promised love and forgiving.
The five-week voyage was full of fun.
We felt our adventure had just begun.

I loved our new home, though things were not quite right.
My husband's cravings became a blight.
He had to go! And go he went.
The relief to me was heaven-sent.
I made a living as a housekeeper for a judge.
But homesickness soon took over and wouldn't budge
But my daughter loved the life, especially riding,
It became a hobby, all-abiding.

She was settled, and wanted to stay
To complete her education, come-what-may.
A life full of fun, with horses to ride,
Experiences that England could never provide.

But I couldn't give up without a fight
And prayed that my decision was right.
On docking at Tilbury, amid familiar sounds,
My love for my daughter knew no bounds.

Moments we shared on our journeys
Will stay with me to my dying day.
To my delight she finally smiled and showed her feelings,
And so my life took on a whole new meaning.

Pat's Story

Australia, half a world away, yet it beckoned to me

Pat

I was born in 1924 and lived in Kensington, London. My father was a boilermaker, and I learned, what was euphemistically termed in those days, a ladies' man. I also learned that my mother fell in love with a submariner, though I'm not sure it was reciprocated! Nevertheless, such romantic dreams had a direct effect on my life. I began courting a young man who for some reason reminded mum of her unrequited love, and she encouraged me to marry him!

Friends and family made every effort to ensure my wedding day was exceptional and memorable, which of course involved hard work and funding. The fund came from our paid employment which was the laborious toil of attaching wire hinges to pieces of wood, which became clothes pegs! So, with tenacity and determination, those pegs provided enough money to dress me in white for the day of the nuptials. One day in 1946, I was fussed into my exquisite (at least, to me) wedding gown and, as was the custom in those days, supplied with a bouquet half the size of my slight self. The fragrance followed me down the aisle to my fate. The all-too-brief honeymoon period was sadly replaced with the realization that my "Romeo" was in fact not just a stoker in the Navy, but that he stoked his own fire with copious amounts of alcohol.

Some nine years later, in 1955, my mother passed away, and without that responsibility, my husband and I, together with our daughter, sailed to Australia on a first class ticket with brand new bungalow awaiting us. We hoped to salvage our already failing marriage.

The five-week voyage was nothing short of breath-taking and we enjoyed the same pleasures as the fare-paying passengers, even being invited to dine at the captain's table. I felt so privileged: it was such an honour. The table was adorned with a crisp white linen, complete with white linen napkins. Crystal glasses and condiments took pride of place with gleaming silver cutlery, and the entire table was enhanced with two bowls of fragrant red roses.

The ship was enormous, in fact, the deck was a mile long, which meant my daughter and I could get plenty of exercise and we squealed with delight when we saw dolphins ducking and diving alongside the ship, putting on a special display just for us. In the evenings we were entertained by live shows and films in the ship's cinema, a different world from anything we were accustomed to. "I could get used to this!" I thought.

There was a spacious house waiting for us on arrival, a new bungalow with three bedrooms. Such luxury. This gave me the courage to rid myself of the drunken husband. Indeed, I sent him packing after a mere few weeks and Lin and I stayed in that superb bungalow for about six months. How free I felt, and I managed to get a job as a cook to support us.

I don't know how I found the courage, but I decided we would have more opportunities if we moved south to New

South Wales, so we took the train from Perth to Sydney, a tiring three-day journey, but one filled with vistas we'd never before seen. And it was in Sydney that I secured a position as housekeeper with a well-to-do judge. Yes, I was to be housekeeper to a judge, a world far removed from the life in England. The house was in fact a seventeen-room mansion and it was here that I became more determined to save our passage back to England. I would be truly free of the husband I had already left. My daughter visited him several times but became distressed and troubled by his behaviour, so this resolved me further to return to England.

The role of housekeeper at the judge's house, provided my daughter and me with a beautiful place to live whilst I earned the money to take us home. As housekeeper, I would dress in a green uniform for day work, and in the evenings, I would don a stiffly starched white apron and had to learn silver service. I would remember the starching for ever as the starch was made from rice water, something new to me, as was the breakfast the judge and his wife ate, which was bread with sugar, a far cry from the appetizing breakfasts I was used to.

The house was situated on a sheep farm in the outback, and although there was a nearby town, I never visited it, being focused on my mission! My daughter, on the other hand, loved the freedom of the great spaces and the horse riding she shared with the judge's children. She was also settled in school and thus was reluctant to leave her new life in Australia. But leave we did, and as we docked at Tilbury, some months later, I couldn't help but compare the grime, the dullness with the brightness and sunshine we had left. However, we were home, and other adventures were awaiting us.

Fragment, Margaret Challans
You can't be faint-hearted to be a scientist

"Only a babe", council-house bred,
"Only a lass", but eleven plus passed,
"Only a girl," nay, a Bachelor's gained –
Five years' hard graft, eyes strained.
Deep curtsy (practised) to the Queen Mum,
Hands proudly accepting, round parchment scroll,
Margaret's degree received, red lips smiling,
At crimson-plush Royal Albert Hall, beguiling.

A slip of a girl, slight and demure,
But, The Rolls Royce of jobs, Derby's best to be sure: metal fatigue was hers to test.
And then did she dive into analysis, inspection: a scientist
Brave-Heart, she strove for perfection,
Though, with a bow to the men,
Those fallen in war, whose shoes she could step in.
Strange odds they had dealt her; small feet in great boots.

"Only a woman", but what did she leave us?
Early cures for goitre, thyroid and cancer;
Radio-Active-Isotope absorption she tested.
Brave woman, only a leather apron protection.

"You can't be faint-hearted to be a scientist," she smiled at her son.
"Your mother's a genius," the doctor-friend praised.
Her legacy till now: radiographers' badges to detect radiation.
What a woman, what a triumph! No under-estimation.

Margaret's Story

Margaret

I've had what I thought was a pretty normal life but on beginning to relate it to others, I have discovered that it was quite a remarkable one; however I will leave you to make up your own minds on this matter.

Life began for me in Derby City Hospital on May 6th, 1934 when I was born to Irene May Wickman and Roger Robson Hodson. We all lived in a council house in Derby along with my brother, who was also called Roger. We had a normal happy childhood with my father working at Rolls Royce and mum being a housewife, but things began to change as I grew older.

In 1945 I passed the "Eleven Plus" examination and went to Homeland's Grammar School. It was here that I began to develop a real interest in maths and scientific studies, so when I left school at 16, I looked around for a job where I could develop my interests and I was lucky enough to obtain work at Rolls-Royce in their science department. At the end of the war, industry was short of qualified workers because of the numbers of men killed during the bombing and fighting, and the Ministry of Education set up a scheme with companies to allow some working hours to be used for education and I was able to attend Derby Technical School in Normanton Road on a day- release scheme. It took five years of sleepless nights and hard study, times of doubt, but at the end I obtained an external Bachelor of Science degree from London University. This was one of the most stimulating moments in my life as I had to go to London to be presented with my degree by Queen Elizabeth, the present queen's mother, at The Royal Albert Hall. Obviously, I had to have a complete new outfit of the latest fashion, and I vividly remember being rather nervous at the thought of curtseying. I was sure I would topple over, but fortunately all went well. I was just twenty-one at the time and all the pomp and ceremony was thrilling.

Returning to Derby was a bit of a let-down but I still had to work for a living, and it was during my time at Rolls-Royce I experimented, amongst other things, on analysis to try to find the causes of metal fatigue resulting from damage by pollution.

I don't know if it was itchy feet that made me apply for a position in Nottingham or just a desire to spread my wings, but whatever, I applied to Nottingham General Hospital to work, precisely, doing research on the use of radio isotopes. This was at a time when women were not easily accepted into the largely male world of research, but I was fortunate in that Dr Miller, the Head of the Sheffield Regional Board, decided to take a chance on me. I was put to work under the Head of the Isotopes Unit, a Mr Rees, a very charming young Welshman.

When I first came to work in Nottingham, I still lived in Derby and this meant I had to get up extremely early to catch a bus and then I was back late at night, so not much time for a social life. It was time, I decided, to move to Nottingham. I lived for a short while at the YWCA on Shakespeare Street but then I was lucky enough to move into a flat with two girlfriends: one who was a policewoman called Sheila, who unfortunately died young of tuberculosis, and my other flat mate was a history teacher. She later went to live in New Zealand, where I have since visited her. It was through one of the other girlfriends I made while working at the hospital that I met the man I was later to marry.

Before I get carried away with the man, (pun intended!) let's return to my research which was on the use of radio isotopes to diagnose problems with the thyroid gland. This treatment had been used for hyperthyroidism since the early 1940's; patients were given a solution to drink, a third of which contained radioactive iodine, diluted, and thankfully, both tasteless and odourless. After a lapse of time, a urine sample was tested to see how much iodine had been absorbed, and these results were then transferred to a graph for analysis. Some patients were averse to taking the liquid and I remember one lady getting very agitated and, to our horror, throwing the glass over her shoulder. The entire contents swam all over the laboratory, and meant we had to shut the whole area down while it was made safe for use. But, thinking back to those times, it was very exciting to be part of a team who were pioneers in the use of radio isotopes, working to find cures for cancers, goitres and thyroid problems, incidentally, no better place for this research than Derby and Nottingham, given the high incidence of goitre, apparently due to being so far from the sea and hence lack of fish and iodine in the diet.

One of the things I remember is that the only protection we radiographers wore was a leather apron, and when one thinks of the amount of protection that is now worn, even by

Margaret

policemen just picking up clues, this seems remarkable. And if we remember the emphasis on good PPE in the time of Covid -19, it also highlights how little emphasis there was on protective equipment in my day. I don't know if it was because I had an inkling that it might be a good idea to know how much radioactivity one's body was absorbing, but I went on to do research on this subject and was instrumental in the making of badges that are worn by radiographers in hospitals to this day!

I found research and work so exciting that I didn't really have time for boyfriends, but when I met Marian Challans, who was a radiographer at the hospital, I was invited to a party at her mum's and literally fell for her brother. He was sitting stretched out on the stairs and I wasn't looking where I was going and tripped over his legs, perhaps a bit of an excessive way to fall in love, but I'm so glad I did. The next time we met, he arrived at my flat carrying a very large toy dog which I have to this day. The dog clinched the relationship!

Martin and I married in 1962, when I was twenty – eight, at St Giles' in Derby and my way of life changed again as married women didn't tend to work in those days.

The next big stepping-stone in my life was the birth of

our children, Mary Jane and Stuart Paul - this meant that I became a stay-at-home mother. What a great change - I was no longer testing urine samples but changing nappies instead.

When we first got married, like many couples, we lived with Martin's parents (on Westview Road) and when the old gentleman next door left, he arranged for them to buy the house for £3,500 and we moved in. I settled down to a life of domesticity.

Time has really flown and it was not until I was on a week's annual holiday with friends from Age Concern Carlton that I happened to tell them about my work on isotopes and the team thought this would make an interesting entry to the book, **A Second Voice** which tells the stories of members' lives. Thus, I try to remember events from my apparently important past.

To return to my working life, when the children were old enough, I became a laboratory technician at Gedling comprehensive school and when the science teacher was taken ill, I was able to teach for a while. I must have done a good job as I was asked to become a full-time member of the staff but I preferred working as a laboratory assistant since this was not so regimented and I could get to know the children who often came to my house for extra lessons in science and maths.

One incident I recall though, whilst doing an experiment, was dropping a bottle of bromide in the laboratory and the entire science department had to be evacuated and I ended up in hospital for the night. You can't be faint-hearted if you're a scientist!

When talking to my son Stuart a little time ago about writing my lifestory he remembered how, when he was a small boy, Dr Miller used to call to see me, and he recalled the gentleman telling him that his mother was a genius. Whilst I can't remember this myself, I am very happy that a learned professor thought enough about me to say it to my son, and I hope that some of the research I have done in my life has been of use.

We cannot underestimate the value of memory and what those memories give to our nearest and dearest. I am very lucky that my son lives close to me so he has been able to help with teasing out those important memories that may, otherwise, have been lost forever.

Fragment, Catherine Clarke

What a loving life we had,
Until our mother took bad.
Endless coughing and losing weight,
Admission to hospital sealed her fate.

Our father was completely vexed,
Trying to decide what to do next.
Kind friends and family came to his aid,
A temporary solution is what they made.

Inevitably, we were sent to a home,
My brothers and I with no place to roam.
A winding path revealed our fate,
A stark gray building, which I learned to hate.

This was to be our abode for years.
So much to digest - no time for tears.
There was no welcome, all seemed old.
My brothers looked lost and shivered with cold.

But mum made up for our life of chaos,
Where tension would sometimes fray us.
And as soon as she was fit and well,
She secured a job, forgetting her hell
Of operations and hospital beds,
Tonics and everlasting meds.

Driving was a dream come true,
As she passed her tests, as well we knew.
This was our mum of whom we were proud,
And extolled her virtues way out loud!

Catherine's Story

Catherine L Philp and John R

My story begins in 1953 when I was six years old, living in Whitby and when my mother succumbed to T.B. She was a kind and considerate woman, but T.B. had no sympathy, and she had been coughing, losing weight and becoming extremely lethargic for some considerable time. Eventually, after her diagnosis, she was admitted into hospital and had half of her right lung removed. My father was devastated, as besides me, he had two small sons, John, three, and Philip, ten months. My friend's mother took me in, Aunt Jenny looked after John, and a kind neighbour helped out with Philip. Of course, these arrangements could only be temporary and before long, we were taken to a children's home in Pickering.

The approach to the home was up a long path, leading to a rather forbidding house of dark grey stone, millstone grit. Years later, I discovered it was originally built as a workhouse, hence the gloomy, cheerless, depressing appearance. It will stay with me forever that some of the staff were hard-hearted, uncaring, even callous. To add to our discomfort, the food was unremittingly awful and I was forced to eat and drink what others may have found wholesome – milky puddings and roast dinner, but to this day, I can't stomach either.

One of the worst things was we missed mum – we had little or no contact with her and only occasionally were we allowed to go to our real home. We were to spend three long years off and on in the children's home. I remember in particular the Christmases there. Sitting in a circle on low wooden chairs, we were handed a small stocking, each of which contained an apple, orange, nuts and a toy. This was not what we had been used to and even the carol-singing couldn't cheer our spirits. But one Christmas I sewed mum a soap pouch from a pink flannel and edged it carefully with blanket stitch, then, with love, slipped inside a fragrant bar of pink Camay soap. Only the best for mum! After all, she was the mother who sent us each a shiny sixpenny bit, carefully wrapped in tissue paper. Very sadly, the home denied us our pocket money because of this. I also thought of dad, and calculated that just one six penny piece would have contributed towards his bus fares to visit mum and us. As it was, he walked and hitch-hiked from Whitby to Pickering and on to York, a distance of forty-seven miles.

I recall that T.B. patients spent all day outside in bed as it was believed that the fresh air, indeed, the bracing air of the North York moors, would cure the illness. I remember very clearly uncle Trevor would drive us to the sanatorium to get a glimpse of mum from a distance. He would stop the car when he could see the building and he and dad would hold us up so we could see mum in her bed on the balcony, then we would wave furiously, our only means of communicating with our beloved mother.

We had to spend three years apart from her, and when mum eventually came home, I was ten. What a joyful moment that was, and unlike many people in that day, she had made a good recovery. I think in part her recovery was due to her strong spirit, which I believe I have inherited, so, she didn't sit home and languish. Instead, she started to fulfil her dream of learning to drive. To this end, she became the proud owner of a green Vauxhall Viva which had belonged to uncle Ralph. Not only did she learn to drive a car, but, with a large helping of determination, she also learned to drive a bus. She became "Whitby's First Driving Gran," so said the headline in the local newspaper, and she drove the forty-five-seater around the villages, picking up school kids! And as if that weren't enough, she became a cook at a rest-home , Sneaton Castle, which supported nuns and monks who had returned from missionary work abroad.

Although the period in the Children's Home was such an upsetting time, once our mother was home, she provided me, Catherine, with an outstanding role model and gave me the strength and courage which has made me the person I am today. Thank you, mum.

Fragment, Rocco Biase Di Martino

We ploughed the fields and scattered
Hopeful seeds, strewn left and right,
An arc, a rainbow of promise, in a flurry of yellow grain.
Grow, grain, grow! silently, we prayed each spring
When handfuls of gold fell furrow-bound, to nestle in the ground.

Parents waited, anxious for growth, of seed, of children,
Children who trudged the furrows, barefoot.
Hard earth felt beneath young toes,
Feet grew calloused as they laboured long.
Then, green shoots strong, pushed to the light, a hope, a blessing, food to delight.

Harvest came with a searing heat, rustling of wheat as warm winds
Fanned the fields, plump with corn and gash of poppy ,
Jingling with sparrow, starling, crow. Now time was ripe to
Scythe, to cut, to whoosh through heavy- headed stalks,
To bundle into sheaves, shirts wet, hands calloused as feet, to harvest this wheat.

Then to the granary did we go, atop the waggon, behind the skinny horse,
Kicking up bone-dry earth, dust and grit in our mouths our eyes our hair,
Iron wheels, the sound of thunder in the air.
Offloading of sheaves was our next intent, and then to hear
Those mill stones grind, to crush the wheat and make us flour, our mama to greet.

Strong hands she had, firm arms, white flour flowing, clouding into large brown bowl.
Slosh in the water, stir, kneed and slap the dough, make the pasta, our bellies to fill.
Next,crimson tomatoes, ripe and round, with onions rich, our taste to thrill.
Joy of harvest, and of rest, smiles amid a family, blessed.
We forgot long days and calloused feet - we sat and ate, ourselves to sate.

Rocco's Story

Rocco in sunny Carlton

I stood up in the small gathering at Age Concern and pointed at my lower leg and the boot I was wearing. "Here." I said, "This is where I'm from!" The faces looked on, blank. "I'm from here," I insisted, smiling wryly. "This is the boot of Italy, and I was born about halfway up, just north of Rome!!" They began to smile as they understood my joke. "I was born in a village called Guardiagrele, in 1932, a village in the foothills of the Maiella mountains.

I will attempt to tell my story as I remember it.

I was the third eldest of six, one sister and four brothers. My family were agricultural labourers, and because we didn't own the land, we were poor, like so many in those small, rural, Italian communities. Our house was a two-storey stone cottage, and as well as sheltering us, it was home to a skinny horse and an ox that pulled the plough.

We were allowed to grow our own food but it was sometimes scarce, though my hard-working mama always made sure we had full bellies, probably full of delicious pasta! Full bellies were essential for bambini who were ever-growing, and essential as most of us had to help papa till the land, even mama had to help!

Another thing I remember was that we didn't have proper shoes, not as we know them today. Instead, we cut soles from tough, old, disused, rubber tyres and strapped them to our feet as best we could. Non ricordo, scusi, I can't quite remember but I think my feet must have been sore and calloused, especially at those times when I had to go barefoot. Indeed, I didn't own a pair of shoes till I was eighteen! Imagine.

Despite the hardships, we were happy children, having loving and loyal parents. As with many children in our region, we had no formal education. The little learning we had came from mama as we sat around our kitchen table.

Papa grew wheat and laboured endlessly in the fields, ploughing with the ox and a hand plough, sowing seed and gathering in the harvest, once the crops ripened in June or July, God willing! At an early age, I was expected to help dad on the land. It was tough, and we had to be up by dawn to avoid the blistering heat of the summer sun. As you can imagine, it was very hot in Italy. The days were long, and so we could finish the day's work, we would resume after the siesta, once the fire had gone out of the day. The ripened golden wheat had to be cut using scythes and bundled into sheaves before the skinny horse pulled the laden cart to the granary where the wheat was milled into flour, probably the very flour that mama made her pasta from. And, so, the cycle continued till the pasta found its way into our bellies.

As I was changing my sheets quite recently in the Covid-19 lockdown, I remembered another thing: our family and most others round and about grew their own flax from seed which was then spun and made into linen bedsheets. Oh, so much work was poured into the land to make those sheets!!

It goes without saying, Italy was a poor country and emigration offered the hope of a better life, so, with the help of my father, who somehow saved for my passage, I followed my eldest brother Antonio to begin an adventure in a land thousands of miles across the sea, a country where millions of Italians emigrated to seek their fortunes. This land was Argentina and at the age of eighteen I was to sail from Naples to Buenos Aires, Argentina, the land of beef and the tango, though I never saw any dancing. It took two weeks to cross the mighty Atlantic, crammed into a cabin with four others and no shower, nevertheless, I remained hopeful of a better life in the building trade.

Rocco's mum and the skinny horse!

The opportunity should have been a great one, but all I remember was a lonely existence in a single room inside a wooden hut in the corner of a building site. This was my "home" for two years as I eked out a living laying bricks. There was a one-ring electric cooker which was my kitchen and the rest of my "home" comprised a single rickety bed, and a hole in the floor was my toilet. No showers here, either, just a nearby lake. Weekends were tedious and lonely as everyone else went home and I had to stay on site to look after the new builds. Fortunately, I remember very little about this period of my life, far from mama and

Rocco in Italian military uniform

papa and in a land where they spoke Spanish, not Italian. As I say, memory is dull here, but I managed to save enough to return to Italy after two years, and to my relief, to repay, papa. On return, military-life beckoned and I joined the Italian army round about 1952.

And so, my life followed the pattern of many – childhood at home, a brief adventure overseas, the military and then marriage, in 1955. Marriage was to my second cousin, and together we came to England in 1956, once again to escape poverty. Initially, I worked the land as I had in Italy but, later, we found other work in Nottingham and Derby. Nottingham has been my home since 1956, and here I sit many a day with friends at Age Concern.

Horse-drawn waggon with essential foods

A 115797

Aliens Order, 1920.

CERTIFICATE OF REGISTRATION

You must produce this certificate if required to do so by any Police Officer, Immigration Officer, or member of His Majesty's forces acting in the course of his duty.

Aliens Order, Rocco

Fragment, Bill and Shirley Godber

The country was in an awful plight
Looking for workers to help win the fight.
Tall, short, fat or hairy,
No one was looked upon un-fairly,
Shirley armed with fork and spade,
Her commitment fully made,
Set forth with vim and vigour,
To do her bit, so she figured.
She joined the Women's Land Army,
Even if it was a bit barmy!

Working in the freezing fields wasn't fun,
But there was potato harvesting to be done.
Fingers now with mud and ice were rigid,
Till mugs of tea thawed frozen digit.
Work was long and hard,
Pulling carrots yard after yard,
Then the end was in sight.
That was the coming of darkening night
And in a cubicle on a hard bunk bed,
This was where she laid her weary head.

Shirley was tall, good looking and full of fun,
She knew how to play when work was done.
Once a week she caught a train into town.
This soon stopped her from feeling down.
Streets were as dark as pitch
But Land Girls knew how to make things tick
And a visit to the Palais de Dance
Could possibly mean a new romance.
However, time flies and soon it was the morrow,

No time for regrets or sorrow.
It was back to the fields, cold and mud
But what Shirley and the girls were doing was for all our good.

We stared in wonder at the envelope.
"Well open it ,you dope," I said to Bill.
"I am, I am!" said he.
The weight and texture of the paper gave Bill quite
A thrill .

Staring over his shoulder,
The excitement made me bolder.
"Is it really? Can it be ?"
"'Ere, pass it over. Let me see."

You could hear our heavy breathing
As we read on, unbelieving.
Our eyes were not deceiving.
Was it really us receiving a letter from
The Queen?

Seventy years of wedded bliss.
I made a sandwich .
"'am or cheese, Bill?"
"'am, please, Ma' am", said Bill.

Bill and Shirley's Story

I'm sure I never imagined when I started on life's journey that one day I would be hanging a letter from the Queen on my wall, but it happened.

Bill and Shirley Godber and, Stephen

I first saw the light of day in my grandmother's house on Bourne Street in Netherfield. Babies were usually born at home - in 1928 there was no National Health, only a midwife and a lot of hot water. My father, William, was a fireman on the railway and not long after I was born, he and my mum, Anne, moved to Colchester. There we lived in a bungalow in a village called West Bergholt, and whilst the surrounding countryside was beautiful, the facilities were back in the Middle Ages, no running water or electricity, so candles and buckets were an absolute necessity. My mum had to go out to work so I spent a lot of time alone, but fortunately we had a kindly neighbour, a Mrs Lee, who used to make sure I ate my dinner which was left on the table, and although this sounds like I was a poor little latch- key child, it wasn't the case because I had a wonderful best friend, a dog called Rover. In 1934, when I was six, we returned to Netherfield, and though I missed the green fields which were replaced with concrete streets and smoking chimneys I did enjoy the comfort of running water and electric lights.

I had a pretty standard education, first at Ashwell Street Juniors and then Carlton Girls. Luckily, our teachers looked upon education as a vocation and what I got as basic lessons would probably get me into university today. There was no choice when you left school-you went to work.

My first job, at the age of fourteen, was at Standen Motors. This company had taken over the Bourne's Factory on Victoria Road during the war and was only minutes' walk from my home. I was to train as a typist at the enormous sum of one pound two shillings and sixpence a week, not much by today's standards, but in those days, you could buy a dream meal of fish and chips with a penneth of bits wrapped in newspaper . No taste today quite compares, and with salt and vinegar it was a little bit of heaven. Luckily, we lived very near to Bestwick's Chip Shop, one of the best for miles around, and on Fridays, there were long queues of women waiting to get a meal that would eke out the week's rations. Life wasn't easy during the war. There was food rationing, air raids and no street lighting which made going out in the evenings quite dangerous. Fortunately for me I loved reading and I also now had a little sister Janice.

Working as a typist was alright but like lots of teenagers I had itchy feet, so in 1945, at the age of seventeen, I joined the Land Army. I thought I would be doing my bit to keep the country going by working on the land, replacing the men who had been conscripted. It wasn't quite the glamorous life I hoped for, but it did have its moments. I was sent to Collingham to a hostel run by a warden of the old school who had Dickensian ideas about young ladies' behaviour. We were squashed two to a cubicle with little privacy, so after an exhausting day in the fields, all you could do was collapse on your bunk and hope to get some uninterrupted sleep. There was very little relief from this knackering routine, except one night a week when we were allowed to stay out until 10 p.m. Sometimes, if we had the strength, we would catch the train to Nottingham or Lincoln to go dancing. One of the real highlights was when we were invited to Swinderby Airforce Base, not only were there handsome young men in uniforms, but more importantly, food. There were always buffets with tempting morsels we didn't get in the hostel, like real ham instead of Spam sandwiches, chocolate goodies, so we used to take paper bags with us and sneak snacks to take back.

Memory is a strange thing and can miss important events, but I do recall that when the war was over and I was still working as a Land Girl that the winter of 1947 was particularly vicious. The arctic conditions made the farmer take pity on us and erect tents with heaters inside so that we could thaw our frozen, chilblained fingers before beginning another "carroting" session. There is little wonder that they gave us a special medal when it was all over.

After leaving the Land Army, I worked for Luxfors, a furniture company in Colwick and while working there I met Bill. In those days we used to arrange to meet boys outside picture houses and my friend had set up a blind date outside the Elite Cinema on Parliament Street, and so in a New Look outfit and feeling rather attractive, we began walking from the bus station. I was quite excited, not knowing who I was going to meet. However, when we got closer to the meeting spot I said to my friend, "Which one is Bill?" One look was enough: he wasn't exactly a Cary Grant look-alike, so I decided to give him a miss and we walked by on the opposite side of the street. But, as time passed, we did arrange to meet again. I had learned a bit more about him and this time it was he who didn't turn up, so I decided to call on his home. When

I arrived, he greeted me with, " What are you doing here?" and my reply was, "It would be more correct to say, what are you doing here, you were supposed to be meeting me for a date an hour ago." And that's how we began our long relationship.

Shirley & Bill Godber Wedding 24 Dec 1949

I made it quite clear that if we were going to get married, then we needed to save some money. You couldn't go to the " social" in those days for a handout, and waiting to get a council house could take years. However, when the time came for our wedding, which was to be Christmas Eve 1949, I asked Bill for his share towards the cost and the reply I got was, "I gave it to my brother Walter because he was in a spot of bother". That was it as far as I was concerned, and I was quite prepared to walk away but Bill was adamant and it was either we got married at Christmas or not at all, so at the age of twenty one, I got married. I wore a beautiful white wedding dress and my two bridesmaids wore green and we had a real family reception at Jacky Bell's. After the reception, we went to Mablethorpe for our honeymoon. Though that may not sound very romantic by today's standards, we were young and full of great expectations for a new life ahead of us.

I didn't really know a great deal about Bill but during our first years together I did pick up snippets about his time in the army and his early life. He was born in Arnold on February

Shirley Godber and Friends

12th, 1926, to Ernest and Mildred Godber. His early years were not very happy as his father was not keen on work and often used to hit Bill when he was a youngster. As soon as he was old enough, he enlisted in the army, that was on February 23rd, 1943 when he was just seventeen. He desperately wanted to join the Sherwood Foresters and asked to be called up as soon as possible after August 12th, 1943 but unfortunately, he didn't make it into the Foresters. Instead, he was posted to the Royal Warwickshire regiment in 1944 after doing his primary training in Lincolnshire and Norfolk. Bill's army record does lead one to believe that he wasn't all that keen on obeying orders. There is a record that he had to pay twenty-one shillings and eight pence fine to make good the ankle boots he had allowed to become unserviceable through neglect. Later in his military career, he was accused of being insolent to a superior officer. This was classed as Conduct to the Prejudice of Good Order and Military Discipline. During his time in the army, he served in France and Germany and was once sent as a runner whilst under fire but by the time he arrived at his destination, he was so scared, he forgot the message. I don't think this went down well with his superiors either and he was finally demobbed in 1947. There was obviously something about army life that was attractive to Bill as he joined the Territorial Army and didn't leave until 1959.

To return to our life together, when we first got married, we lived in rooms in Sherwood but when our son Steven was born, we moved in to live with my parents in Forester Street. The house was classed as a family house but it only had two bedrooms as one had been converted to a bathroom, and as my sister was still at home, there wasn't enough room for us to sleep in the house, so we had to sleep on the next road in Wallet Street. This wasn't an ideal situation with a baby in arms and some nosy parker neighbour told the authorities that we were living there. Although we knew the owner,we were classed as squatters and told to get out. It meant that I spent a lot of time out on the streets with Steven in the pram and then we would creep back like thieves in the night to sleep. Fortunately, the gentleman who owned the house heard of our plight and came home to stay and let us live with him, which we did for six years until we got a council house in Redland Grove. We lived in this house, our first proper home together, for ten years before exchanging it for one in Cavendish Road.

Shirley Godber

When we were first married, Bill worked at a company called Elastic Yarns for very poor wages, but he was a grafter and would take on any work there was, even at night, and as soon as we could get Steven into a nursery, I went to work as well.

My first job was at the Soap Works but I only lasted six weeks. The forewoman took a dislike to me, possibly because I was quite a lively soul and used to like singing, especially to my friend across the factory. My speciality was "When I'm calling you", so I didn't really mind when they got rid of me because it was a rotten job. I had heard they wanted workers at the hairnet factory under Baker's Arch on Emery's Road which was very convenient for me as it was near to Steven's nursery. Unfortunately, this job was slave labour. You had to card hundreds of hairnets for a few pence, so to make ends meet, I did a temporary job as a sorter at the Post Office as well. Then I got my lucky break: a permanent position became available and I remained there for fifteen years. I became a sort of fixture and even got to take my granddaughter with me sometimes.

Time was fast approaching when we were thinking about retirement and I would have liked to live in Mablethorpe but Bill didn't fancy that and we heard from an old friend that there were some great new properties going in Scunthorpe. I can't say I was very enamoured at the thoughts of moving to a predominately industrial town, but the house did prove to be lovely: the only snag was that the people were not. I had been used to having friendly neighbours and people to talk to and our neighbours in Scunthorpe were the keeping-up-with-the-Joneses variety for the most part. So when our son's marriage broke up, we came back to live with him in Gedling in 2004.

Shirley and Bill

I am still living with my son in his lovely bungalow in Bakerdale Avenue, but sadly Bill passed away in 2020. I am very lucky that I have three grandchildren and eight great-grandchildren plus lots of happy memories of my varied life, and to top it all, after seventy years of marriage, I've got that letter from the Queen to prove it.

Fragment, Jean Jayne Wells

Now is the hour Little John
Spangles of rainbow lights fly
Across a fluid tract
Play chase with sun.

Pigeons billing and cooing amid
Shop signs swoop suddenly
And the old man casts crumbs
Across chewing-gum-pocked Slab Square.

Left Lion guards marble walls
Lustrous silky gossamer ripples
Before him to spring to snatch
To grab but not today

Symbolic figures gaze down
Frozen in time their office
To perform.

Pastel shades of my past
Like confetti scatter
Bridal wreath laughter shimmering
Demure
Memories to cling to.

Jean's Story

Jean

Looking out from my sheltered spot outside Debenhams, I gazed across towards Nottingham's "Slab Square." It had changed over the years since I had moved here. Now there was a large open space, the water features had been re-located to the far end of the square, towards The Bell Inn, and what used to be Yates's Wine Lodge, was now a Slug and Lettuce bar-cum-restaurant.

I shivered slightly in the cool, early-morning air. Clutching my handbag close to me, I remember being told, "Never leave your handbag open when you're standing in Long Row. Men will think you're on t' game!" I, in turn, had told my daughter Gail not to wait by Nottingham's famous Left and Right Lions – another pick-up place.

I always prided myself in my appearance: good clothes and being well-kempt, the former by keeping up with fashion, the latter, thanks to a good stylist. My complexion looked creamy too, despite the odd cigarette and drink.

Out of the corner of my eye, I glimpse something bright blue floating in the air. It's a scarf; a young girl wearing a beautiful sari is trying to gather the scarf to her, laughing as the breeze gently tosses the fabric above her head as she passes into the shelter of the Council House. Her female companions quickly gather round, ushering her forward. She lowers her head, demurely pulling the scarf closer to hide her hair.

The scene immediately transports me back to the days when I worked as a registrar, presiding over the marriage ceremonies of "foreign" couples, first at the Bristol office and then in Nottingham. It seemed many years ago.

Jean

Because of the war, my parents decided it would be safer for my sister Caroline and me to move to our grandparents in Dalbeattie, Scotland. It was easy to settle in with them as we loved them dearly and I enjoyed delivering the savoury meat pies and soft-fruit flans oozing with sweet raspberries or plump tangy gooseberries, all made by gran's friends. I would cycle off, laden with the goodies and folk were so grateful as these were extra rations. The way back always took longer as I lost myself in the tranquil scenery and the gentle sighing of the wind through the trees. Everything here was new and fascinating, including watching grandad in the hot dirty smithy where he laboured as a blacksmith.

It was decided that I would attend De Bere College to learn Greg shorthand which I picked up relatively quickly. Granny saw this as a stepping - stone into the world of work where she hoped I would become a secretary. I remember writing to my parents one evening about my studies and how I thought they were making me speak more clearly. I was surprised by the reply I got. My father, who knew nothing about further education, said shorthand sounded like a secret code and I should be careful. Conversely, mother said she was glad that at last someone would be able to understand me! The effect on me was that it made me determined to grasp every

Jean

chance to prove myself, despite the war. Granny was right, there was a world out there and I had the right to be part of it. The whole experience of education was liberating and the friendly arguments with other girls opened my eyes to a new way of thinking.

However, the world of work proved a little tricky for a now efficient secretary. I only lasted a month in the first job as my tidy ways were not in keeping with their sloppy ones, desks strewn with paper, to say nothing of the cigarette stubs piled in ashtrays.

But these were the war years, and as men were called up, women stepped into jobs previously staffed by them. I went from The Bristol Cream Sherry company to working for a social worker, the latter giving me experience in dealing with the general public.

My big opportunity came when I picked up a newspaper on the train. Someone's loss was my gain. As I scanned the pages, I caught sight of a job advertisement. The position was for a registrar in Bristol. The applicant would have shorthand skills, be well-spoken and enjoy working with people. Just up my street! So, I dug around in my handbag and found the four large pennies I would need for a phone call. As I jumped off the train and headed for the phone box, I could see someone was using it. I felt so impatient, and as he left, didn't want to engage in conversation with this person who spoke to me in Gaelic, but he'd left his notebook in the kiosk and speak we did, albeit briefly. I was already rehearsing my best English accent to impress the person at the other end of the line. The call resulted in a local interview and before I knew it, I'd been offered the job. How would I tell my family that I needed to relocate to Bristol as a registrar working at Quaker Friar's and what's more, in my own flat! Such freedom for a young girl was exhilarating.

On the other hand, I needed to soften the blow to my grandparents who had been so kind. Nothing like some flowers and grandad's favourite tipple to do that, so I stopped off at the local shop on my way home. Fate sometimes surprises you, and who should be serving in the shop but the Gaelic-speaking chap from the phone box. As we chatted, he asked if I'd like to go for a celebratory drink. "You'll have to improve your English," I joked, blushing. Relationships then were intense as we never knew what would happen, and quickly, Steve and I became close, sharing many interests. In fact, the man in the phone box became my dear husband. We had two wonderful children and after he died, I missed him so much and still dream about him.

Jean

As for the day job, I took it and learned so many skills, delivering in clear English to people who spoke little English, the rules of the British marriage ceremony. It was a time of mass immigration.

My mind wandered back down the years, recalling our happy times, also thinking, "Could we have done things better?" But then, when I see my children getting on with their lives, Steve's voice comes to me, soft but clear, "Relax, enjoy them. We did a grand job, Jean."

"Mum, mum," I heard. It was my daughter. The blue scarf had whisked me back in time to when I'd been a registrar at the Council House. As my daughter took my arm, I turned one last time to look at that same grey stone building. The young bride-to-be had gone, but my memories stay, just waiting to be awoken by a glance, a smile, ...a scarf.

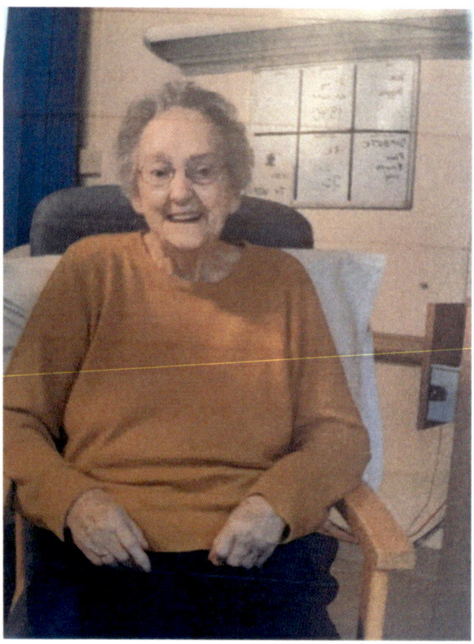

Jean

Fragment, Alan Hughes

I've lived my life throughout the years,
And had my share of joy and tears.
I've done most things that fate decreed,
But one ambition took the lead.
'To fly,' that's what I aimed to do,
Follow on the wartime 'Few.'
So, called to serve at the King's behest,
I trained alongside Britain's best,
Young chaps whose purpose was to fly,
Unstick the earth, take on the sky,
Ensure the Air Force would endure,
A force to keep us all secure.

The years have passed, we've now grown old.
Times have changed, but memories hold -
Of yesteryear and all its cares.
We've had our day, and now it's theirs.

When I sit and reminisce and watch the world go by,
Today's young chaps are taking off and learning how to fly.
They're keeping up the work we did, all those years ago.
I wish them well and hope they continue to do so

Alan's Story

In 1947, faced with National Service, I submitted my name to the Forces Selection Panel to train for aircrew duties within the RAF. My request being granted, I was summoned to RAF Hornchurch near Romford in Essex to undergo aptitude and further medical tests to assess my suitability for the service and, if successful, which part of the aeroplane I would sit in.

Alan relaxing at RAF Heany, near Bulawayo, Southern Rhodesia

One hundred and sixty-two of us in total were put through the procedures but only about 7% were selected for pilot training, happily, including me.

When the call came to report for commencement of training at RAF Cardington, Bedford, I, together with an assembly of other hopefuls, arrived to be kitted out with uniform and service number and to be informed as to where training would take place. Out of the various flying training schools both here and abroad, I was included in a group of sixty future colleagues, eventually heading for No.4 FTS based near Bulawayo in Southern Rhodesia.

The next moves were postings to RAF Hednesford, Staffordshire and Kirton Lindsey in Lincolnshire to be supplied with our overseas khaki kit and flying suits. We were then sent on embarkation leave prior to heading to Southampton to join the Stirling Castle liner to Cape Town.

A fortnight's cruise lay ahead of us and most chaps determined to make the most of it. This had unfortunate consequences for a couple of the guys who gleefully headed for a house of ill repute in Funchal, Madeira, the only stopover on the cruise, and brought back to the ship more than they'd bargained for! Short careers for them when later exposed during routine medical inspections!

The Lads

The 'Crossing the Line' ceremony, an initiation for those crossing the equator for the first time, took place in and around the ship's swimming pool. One lad dressed as Father Neptune was perched on his throne with another, disguised as his Queen Salacia, beside him. They were accompanied by characters dressed in various costumes, overseeing the proceedings. Victims, or 'Tadpoles,' were daubed with a soluble gunge and ceremoniously dumped into the pool to cleanse them from the 'dirt of the north.' It was all good entertainment, especially when a couple of the victims who 'accidentally' lost their trunks, emerged from the water full frontal facing a bemused ship's captain's wife. Other ladies peering through their fingers, expressed mock horror, but were obviously enjoying the spectacle.

Arriving in Cape Town, we were billeted in the Castle, an old 17th century bastion fortress, under the watchful eye of the South African Army based there. A leisurely three days were spent taking in the sights. The wonderful Botanical Gardens and a trip up to the top of Table Mountain via the cable car to sit on Smut's rock were highlights of the visit. Whilst there, we were advised not to appear in public in uniform as there was still evidence of an anti-British attitude from the Dutch descendants of the Voortrekkers who appeared to think the Boer war was still being fought. One notorious spot advised to avoid was District 6 near the docks. The apartheid problem didn't help either.

We still had another couple of days' train journey to Southern Rhodesia via Mafeking and Johannesburg, an experience in itself. Arriving in Bulawayo, we were met by RAF transport and journeyed to our home for the next eighteen months, No.4 Flying Training School based at Heany, several miles to the east of Bulawayo. Heany was equipped with Tiger Moths, Avro Anson and NA Harvard aircraft: anticipation of what was to come was high. A 'stand-down' time of a few days was allowed, due the elevation of the airfield at a heady 4,680 feet, for the intake to acclimatise to the thinner atmosphere before the commencement of duties.

The first six months of the eighteen-month course were lecture-oriented and covered such items as aerodynamics, basic navigation, Air Force Law, physics, pyrotechnics and English, (as she is spoke!) to name but a few. Also, route marches into the Bundu were part of the programme. One trek to 'World's View,' the site of the grave of the founder of Rhodesia's, Cecil Rhodes, was a memorable highlight.

I was billeted with fourteen other chaps known as C Flight, and one, "John" was a nice fellow but he had a habit of returning to quarters after lights out and disturbing his colleagues with his noisy preparations for bed, ignoring pleas to 'Pipe down, John.' This got to the stage where action was taken to teach him a lesson. A condom was gradually filled with water until it contained about 1.25 gallons (yes, unbelievable, but true!). This was duly tied off and suspended from the centre roof beam with enough leeway to very gently move it across and anchor it to the shelf opposite John's bed. Arriving after lights out and performing his usual auditory assault on the ears of the everyone, "John" was allowed to get into bed and nod off. The chap in the bed opposite then released the water bomb, which swung across and burst on hitting the shelf above our miscreant's bed, soaking him. Then all hell broke loose. "John" grabbed a foam fire extinguisher and wildly sprayed the inside of the billet until it looked like an arctic wilderness. Blankets and other objects were suspended from the cross beams and bed frames were upturned. A short time later, the station adjutant, accompanied by a trio of RAF police, burst in and put the place under lockdown. All fourteen of us appeared before the Group Captain C.O. the following morning to have the riot act read to us. "I will

Alan Hughes

not tolerate this ungentlemanly behaviour on my patch," he stormed. "I realise you've been under pressure regarding your studies and you have to let off steam occasionally. There are limits, however. If it wasn't for the fact that the RAF has invested a lot of money to get you this far, you would be on the next boat home." He then added, "You can of course expect additional charges on your mess bills to cover the cost of repairs and replacements." We paid up with relief, realising how close we'd sailed to the wind. High jinx activities are one thing...damage to government property in the process is another.

Having said that, two of our contingent had a good night out in Bulawayo, drinking the local Castle and Lion lagers to excess. Without considering the consequences, after missing the RAF bus back to camp, they hijacked a local fire engine, crashing it, coming off the A5 onto the link road to camp and wrecking it just prior to reaching camp. They apparently intended to park up and abandon it and walk the final distance, but the crash put paid to that. The local police handed them over to the custody of the RAF and they were quickly repatriated to the UK to be dealt with by military court- martial, two more careers wrecked by irresponsible behaviour. We never did learn what became of them.

One of our team, "Eric", (again, name changed), was related to a Pilot Officer Instructor on the camp. On stand-downs, three of us arranged with him to fly in a chartered Airspeed Oxford from Kumalo airfield on the outskirts of Bulawayo to Salisbury and other venues. These flights gave us the opportunity to visit sites we probably would never have seen otherwise. Ndola in Northern Rhodesia was a particularly interesting place and we wished we'd had more opportunity to extend our visits there. The runway at Kumalo, from what I recall, had a sewage farm at one end and a cemetery at the other. It was joked that if things went wrong on take- off or landing, you could literally either end up in the sh**e, or permanently gain your real wings.

On leave to Nairobi in Kenya, a small party of us learned that the filming of 'King Solomon's Mines' was on location at Machakos to the south of Nairobi. Taking a couple of hours' ride in a clapped-out taxi, we arrived on set, to be denied entry until Stewart Granger, learning we were British Nationals and servicemen, welcomed us aboard. A few social hours in the presence of Stewart Granger, Deborah Kerr and Richard Carlson, plus observing the filming of scenes, made our visit worthwhile and pleasurable. Even after all these years, when viewing the film on television, it triggers nostalgia.

Heany had its 'graveyard' where wrecks and other redundant aircraft parts were dumped. Browsing through it one weekend, an abandoned Standard Vanguard car was discovered and rescued by the lads. It was in a bad way body-wise, the paintwork down to the primer in large patches, the small back windows and engine bonnet cover missing. The tyres were badly worn, and the engine needed resurrection. We bribed one of the fitters from the maintenance unit to get the engine running, although it did a lot of backfiring as the A/R mechanism on the distributor was knackered. It was christened in silver paint 'PIEBALD' on both sides, due to its patchy paintwork. We had fun running it around the airfield inner-perimeter and very occasionally, a short distance on the link road connecting us to the A5 when opportunity allowed. It was a bit sluggish on acceleration, so "Eric", after a particularly bad run said, "I'll smarten the bugger up," and purloined a couple of pints of high-octane aviation fuel and poured it in the tank. The result was it ran for about 300 yards before the engine disintegrated in a cloud of black smoke and a small fire, quickly extinguished. The outcome was a severe bollocking from the flight commander and another stiff mess bill appendage to cover the cost of removal of the remains back to the graveyard and the clean- up required on the spot where it died.

RAF pilot-survival training

As training intensified, the adventures lessened, primarily due to lack of leisure time and increasing pressure of the flying factor for which one had to be A1 at all times. On completion of training, the return to the UK for personnel to be dispersed by postings to differing operations and activities was implemented. Friendships formed in Rhodesia faded as the years progressed, but the UK had added another consignment of young men to follow in the footsteps of 'The Few.' Heany was disbanded in January 1954. Today, No.4 FTS continues at RAF Valley in Anglesey.

One follow-up incident which occurred later in April 1958 was the testing of a Scorpion experimental rocket engine fixed in the bomb bay of Canberra WT207 taking off from Hemswell RAF station in Lincolnshire. It was designed to boost the aircraft to a height unobtainable by the normal jet engines. At 56,000 feet, (almost eleven land miles) the Scorpion exploded, ejecting both pilot and navigator out of the disintegrating aircraft above Monyash in Derbyshire. This set the then record for the highest emergency ejection from an aircraft. Both pilot and navigator survived and, following hospital treatment for frostbite and decompression injuries, were eventually allowed to resume flying duties. The pilot, Peter, was a friend of mine whilst training together on No 11 course at Heany in Rhodesia. Although I had no contact with him for many years, I believe he flew as a captain with Caledonian Airways, later British Airways, on leaving the RAF. He passed away in 2005.

The RAF of yesteryear differs greatly from the present-day force, but the Esprit De Corps remains the same.

Fragment, Violet Leivers

The bells rang on our wedding day with such a joyous chime.
The church was lit with happy smiles
As John and I walked down the aisle
To greet that sunny Christmas eve in 1949.

No long white wedding gown for me,
No veil nor sparkling headband.
Coupon-shortage scuppered that,
And so I wore a suit and hat,
A blissful smile, new wedding band,
And fresh-plucked flowers in my hand.

Thus began our lives entwined, our future as yet to be defined.
I bore a son- we had just one,
To guide and cherish throughout his life.
He in his turn found a wife to start his own love story.

Hobbies, work and charities filled up those busy years
Also, grief and sacrifice, and coping with the not-so-nice...
The tolerance, fun and laughter made John
A little dafter to coax some sunshine
Back to lift the heavy weight of tears.

Soon foster children filled our home with noise and boisterous laughter.
We had such fun. They kept us young,
Then one by one, they all moved on to find their happy-ever-after.

Sixty- seven years we had of love and happy banter

Until the day John lost his fight and drifted off into the Night
to leave my heart an empty shell.
I lost the man I'd loved so well.

Now I must wait until I can be with again that loving man,
To feel once more his strong embrace, his gentle lips upon
my face.
Then hand-in-hand we will be spun into eternity.

Violet's Story

My parents, Fred and Lily Towle, lived in Kimberley where dad was a miner and mum stayed home to look after the family. Then, in early 1920, when the miners worked short time, dad decided to move the family, at the time, just my siblings aged eight and sixteen, to Yorkshire, where work was plentiful.

I entered the world a small and delicate baby in the merry month of May, the 13th to be exact, in Stainforth, Yorkshire where we lived in 1926. Then due to dad having an accident in the pit, we moved back to Nottingham, first to Beeston, then to Carlton, then on again to Standhill Road, Carlton where I still live in the family home.

After labouring many years in the dark, dank mines, wrenching coal from the reluctant seams, dad opened a fish and chip shop on the site which eventually became Rex Robinson Cycles, opposite Carlton Square car park, but recently, the crumbling black and white fronted building, home to many pigeons, was demolished.

Childhood for me was a happy time, and in days of seemingly endless sunshine, when I wore only a cotton dress, knickers and sandals, I would play hopscotch and whips and tops with the girls, both games being embellished into fancy patterns by using brightly coloured chalks. I also enjoyed playing marbles with the boys!

In 1939 we were plunged into a brutal war. One day, when I was about thirteen, my family and I were attending the funeral of two neighbours who had been killed during an air raid. As the heavy coffins were borne into the church, we heard the dreaded rumblings of the approaching Messerschmitts. The coffins were abandoned on the grass as the bearers and mourners raced for cover.

I was holding the hand of Harry, a small boy who had been crippled by polio.
"Run!" I yelled at him.
"I can't run fast," he cried, in a voice of rising panic. "You know I can't," as we heard not far behind us, the coffins being peppered with bullets.

I was determined to keep Harry safe. There was no time for fear: we moved as fast as his weak, heavily-booted legs would carry him. We reached our sanctuary and I pushed in the terrified little boy and stumbled in myself, only to hear, seconds after the door had been slammed shut, the bullets hammering on the shelter and the area around us. The noise was deafening, but as it subsided, I could only hear Harry sobbing. We had been so close to death, but for now, we were safe. Our guardian angels were really working overtime on that day. Harry Rolfe matured to be a singer, a top tenor with a very fine voice.

To return to my family story, dad, who was born in 1885 and had served in the Boer War as a horse-mounted despatch rider, developed bronchial pneumonia through working in the mines and died in 1943, aged only fifty-eight. At this point, mum went out to work in the Co-op greengrocery department.

I had always dreamed of becoming a tailoress, but with dad's sad demise, there was not enough money to pay for my training. Consequently, my first job was in Rose's shoe shop, followed by a spell in a chip shop at night and the hateful laundry in the daytime to raise enough cash to pay for my apprenticeship. Determined I was to fulfil my dream of becoming a tailoress!

The yard at the back of the laundry was also a lunchtime refuge for the staff of an engineering company, A. L. Marshall, and because I had been a delicate child, I always took a pint of milk to sip during the day. Gradually, I became aware of a good looking but rather shy young man who always seemed to be looking at me. One day, he approached me and asked if he might have some milk for his tea. We soon became well-acquainted and one day later, he invited me to go to the pictures. I happily agreed because I really liked him, but then again, he could be quite rude to me, which I found confusing. We were content in each other's company, until one day, I told him I wouldn't see him again.
"But, why?" he asked, dismayed. "What have I done?"
"Well, sometimes you say hurtful things to me."
He laughed and explained that was his odd sense of humour and if I could get used to it, he would love me even more than he did then! So, that's how John Neville Leivers declared his devotion to me, and on a bright and sunny Christmas Eve in 1949, we were married at St Cyprian Church, 11 a.m. sharp, with a reception at the Co-op function rooms in town. Because we needed coupons for clothes in those days, I decided to design and make my own wedding outfit, a two-piece suit, mustard with complimentary accessories, and from our garden, I plucked creamy chrysants, my bouquet. A wonderful day, but not without a tinge of sadness as dad wasn't there to give me away or to share the fun afterwards. But like so many who had gone before us, we exchanged our

vows and thus began a lifetime of love and happy banter. John settled seamlessly into our family home where we cared lovingly for my mother through her crippling stroke and frightening loss of memory until the day she finally lost her hold on reality, and weary and confused, she finally passed away.

Violet wearing her medal with pride

After recovering from the loss and time-consuming care of my mother, I sauntered through many empty hours until I was prompted to join a worthwhile cause. I applied to join the W.R.V.S., where I worked for a long time, mostly in Her Majesty's prison, Nottingham, then, after twenty-six years, I was awarded a medal for long service. John also became the proud recipient of two awards, one for completing his National Service, and the second for serving with the British Forces in Germany. Now, on special occasions such as Armistice Day, I proudly wear all three medals, mine on my left shoulder, and John's on my right side for the march past, though nowadays, it's more likely to be a "scooter past"!

At a similar time to joining the W.R.V.S., the leader of Porchester Scout Group, a Mr Carver-Smith, was retiring and looking for a replacement. John applied and was given the post, I became Akala and when our first son, Alex, was

Violet (left) and The Charmaines

old enough to join, we called him Sher Khan, from **Jungle Book**, just in case you didn't know.

We had great fun taking the lads camping to Skeggy, Walesby Forest and Buckmore Park. I cooked and John organised the team games and the boys learned to sew on a button, make tea and generally look after themselves.

If all that wasn't enough, I formed a singing trio, thus fulfilling another of my loves. We called ourselves The Charmains and that song became our signature tune. We entertained mainly in retirement homes but once we sang our hearts out in the Albert Hall, Nottingham. With my light soprano voice I liked to sing songs from the old musicals: Maid of the Mountains; Oklahoma; Rose Marie; and there was nothing better than when the audiences wanted to join in with renditions of Daisy, Daisy; Keep the Home Fires Burning; A long way to Tipperary; which we changed to It's a Long Way to Tickle Mary! What fun.

At 72, I took on my last job which was organising the mother and toddler group at St. John's Church, on Standhill Rd, until I finally retired at 75. And now, aged 92, I zoom around on a mobility scooter, to Age Concern for my lunch and Foxhill Rd Church for the coffee mornings. Scooting is the only way to travel!

Currently, when not bombing along at four miles per hour (the Sterling Moss of Standhill), I spend much time in my peaceful garden, weather-permitting, where I grow strawberries, onions, green beans, and plump tomatoes. I also have a passion for exotic delicately-coloured orchids, which I grow and display on my living room window sill for any visitor to admire, as often they do.

Just another few things before I finish. John and I were happily married for sixty-seven years, and, oh, how I loved that man! He and our boys were my world, and on our sixtieth and sixty-fifth wedding anniversaries we received congratulatory letters from Her Majesty, The Queen, whose two photographs are proudly displayed on the wall of our house.

We had two sons, one we adopted, and from those children we have five grandchildren and five great grandchildren, plus many youngsters we fostered when we needed to fill our time! Someone recently asked me how I would like to be remembered,

"Just as an ordinary woman," I replied.

"Oh, no, Violet. I could never describe you as an ordinary woman," came the reply.

When John died a mere four years ago, a wooden bench was placed in the garden for the blind at the corner of Albert Avenue, and unveiled by our then M.P., Vernon Coaker. I still miss John so much and keep his ashes in a vase in the hall where I talk to him every day, often berating him for leaving me. So, when I eventually reach the Pearly Gates, where

John has probably set himself up (always having a finger in every pie) as assistant gate-keeper, I know he'll be pleased to see me, and I'm equally sure of what he'll say,
"Oh, no. Here she comes. Now my peace will be shattered!"

Needlepoint thank-you to Violet and John

Fragment, Ann Parten

Since Bronze Age, man has thatched his home
With withy rods and good wheat straw
Tied in bundles to make good ridgeline
Longer reed makes good thick thatch
For a good brow, they say Norfolk reed be best.

Climb my ladder. The woodpigeon
Gives his applause as he claps away
From his perch
Below, the heron watches, walking
By the river bed.

Falling, reeds pull me down
Rain don't stop
Legs hurt
Climb back up, carry on.
Thought I was gone.

Not a people person.
My principles are high
Reputation's my creed.

Once a poor-man's shelter,
A status symbol.

Keep reed beds neat
Cut don't burn.
Think of wild life.
Learn!

Ann's Story

I'll begin with the "hearsay" things, but I don't think I'll be able to keep the tales in chronological order.

Perhaps it was because I was the youngest of four children that I tended to spend most of my baby/child years with adults. Mother was always busy earning the butter to go on the bread – dad earned only enough for the basics like rent, coal, gas (for cooking and light), clothes and food. Dad wasn't afraid of work. After a full day in the factory, he'd work the large garden and allotment so we never went short of fresh vegetables. And from scraps, mainly vegetable peelings and undersized vegetables boiled down to mash, about four hens, (and at Christmas, a couple of cockerels), were always there to keep us in eggs.

Dad was a skilled engineer, operating a milling machine, so heaven knows how the labourers managed. Of course, mother was never allowed to see his pay packet and she had to manage on whatever he gave her. He always took out his betting money, and enough to go to football every week. Mother said she only heard of the bets that came up, never the losses.

We all had jobs to do round the house so that mother could spend the whole day "gloving". She made and lined Dent's gloves. I was left with Olive, eight years my senior, to be looked after. At weekends Granny Pom (mother's mum) and Granfy Pom, her second husband, walked into Yeovil from whichever of the surrounding villages they happened to be living in at the time. From them, I had the only loving I can remember.

Always, they brought a big cake or pie. Sometimes, Pom had caught a couple of rabbits, or had scrounged a "pluck" (heart liver and lungs) from a pig that had been killed. This meant that the family's meat intake was doubled and we had a feast. Without granny's treats, food would have been very dull. Mother hated cooking, and the lovely vegetables that dad grew were boiled and slapped on the plate, and that was it!

Granfy Pom always cuddled me and took me for walks in fine weather. When we couldn't get out, I spent hours on his knee, listening to his stories. "You don't want to yere that, maid", but he would always tell me the tale. We were both "in the way" while mother did the Saturday clean and wash, so I expect that was part of the bond between us. I remember Pom as an island of calm and love in a hectic world, too busy to be bothered with a small old-fashioned child who lived in a world that was needlessly interesting.

Pom was a young man some years after the Tolpuddle Martyrs, but the Agricultural Labourers' Union was still frowned upon. He was very pro-union, so his life was made uncomfortable by the farm owners. He was moved on from farm to farm when he tried to claim the so-called basic wage. But he was a many-skilled man, winning prizes for hedging, ploughing, thatching which made him attractive to many farmers as they liked to hire a man who won prizes. He would take whatever pay he was offered, but once settled, he would agitate for his rights. Many owners sneaked away from the minimum wage by charging for the perks that had always been free – "skilly" (skimmed milk) and gleanings from the fields after harvesting.

Pom had eight children by his first wife, but he rarely

mentioned them. He rarely mentioned them, so I felt special, and I was his "pert" (pretty one), probably the only one who enjoyed listening to him.

On the farm, harvest was not only the busiest time but also a time of fun and satisfaction. Hay-making was backbreaking for the men who worked side-by-side, scything – step, swing, step swing...all the way across the field, then wheeling around and all the way back again. The bigger children raked the hay into tidy lines to dry. Stone jars of cider were tucked into the shadow of the hedges to drink with bread and cheese and there were bottles of cold tea, very nice too, to quench the thirst of the workers.

Pom the Warlock

One great tale was the "folklore" of how Pom gained his reputation for being a warlock. He had won a West of England prize for thatching. This earned him a few shillings, but the farmer had the kudos and trophy, so Pom thought he'd try his luck for a rise. Instead of a good result, Pom was told he was "out, come Michaelmas!" The farmer promptly decided to make a good water-tight thatch on the hayrick. Pom was heard to say, I hope he falls breaks his neck!" Indeed, the farmer did fall, though, fortunately, broke only his leg... but it was enough to start the whisper of Pom having the evil eye! He and his family were hastily put out of their cottage and had to disperse among relatives for two or three months until hiring day the

Granny Pom

following Michaelmas.

Now, the poor man was a warlock as well as being a rabble rouser! His calm fun is best illustrated by the story of "Granfy Pom and the Teapot."

Remember, dear reader, washing was a major task. Tablecloths were always white and had to be boiled to get them white, rinsed in Dolly-Blue-dip to get them extra white, starched, dried on the clothes line, damped and rolled down and finally ironed! Quite a performance.

Well, the teapot in question seemed to have a faulty spout and it dribbled. I expect that a spot or two on a clean cloth was the last straw, and Thirza's (granny Pom) temper got the better of her. She stepped out of the back door and yelled, "Bliddy thing!! And chucked the teapot over the hedge. Pom happened to be coming home when the pot, spewing boiling water, landed at his feet. When he entered the kitchen, he quietly placed the pot on the table and said, "'Spec' you'll need this, maid."

Pom told of the hardships of the day – it was rare for a man to live to his allotted three score years and ten, and women looked old by the age of forty-five or fifty. It was common to hear of men outliving two or three wives as many died having had very large families. Pom's generation was probably the first of the families to have a better than seventy per cent chance of survival. It was usual to lose two or three babies from childhood ailments that were much more severe because of widespread under-nourishment. He died from cancer when he was eighty. In the 1940's, that was old!

Ann Parten 2

- In Thirza's time a family size of twelve to fifteen was the norm. Indeed, she had been one of fourteen, all boys, except for her, so she never went out to work; instead, she had to stay home to look after her father and brothers with her mother. By the time Lydia was having her family it had reduced to about four in the class of people with education but labourers had between six and eight.

- Babies had eight white cotton gowns and two dozen nappies. Boiling was a once-a-week job so that meant three nappies plus one gown a day, i.e. seven in the wash and one on!

- On the other hand, older children were fortunate if they had three of everything. Imagine the pong! It's no wonder the drawers were navy blue!!

- In Thirza's age group, women were still dying in child-bed, though child-bed fever was just beginning to be understood. About one in five babies died before reaching school age; this wasn't always the disaster it would be today. For many families, it was a relief to have one less mouth to feed. Women stayed in bed for ten days if they had a caring family, or got up the next day and went back to work if they were alone in the world. Feeding the baby was thought to be natural birth control and some breast-fed for two or three years. Widespread use of the condom and/or Dutch Cap didn't come about until the 1920's, but even then, they were not very safe methods.

- Lydia was married in 1914 and had her first child in 1915. Women began to taste freedom during the Great War. Middle class women fought hard to educate their "sisters" so that they could fend for themselves. In fact, many did he jobs of their own men-folk with a view to keeping the job open for the man to come back to.

- Lloyd George's Shilling, the first old-age pension, came in about 1908/9, I think, but you still had to pay if you visited the doctor, though some industrial areas had a 3d-a-week welfare doctor, in which case you had only to pay for the medicine.

- Operations like tonsil extractions or setting a broken leg were done on the kitchen table; teeth were pulled after a glass or two of gin; hospitals were places to die in; cross-infection was rife. Tonsils were only extracted in hospital if your father had paid into a fund. I was done in about 1934 at 10 a.m. and was home, still dopey, at about 2 p.m.

- As far as I know, no working man had a bank account before the Second World War. If you had nay spare cash, you might have a Post Office book or War Bonds.

- Holidays were just an odd day at the seaside or a family picnic. Sunday School treats were often the highlight of the year and Harvest Home was a royal knees-up!

- Except for miners, who bathed every day, families usually bathed once a week - first father, then mother, then kids in order of age - all in the same water!!

- Washing powder came in between the wars. I can remember grating bars of yellow soap for the washing as late as 1936. Lux flakes were available but very expensive; they were only used for Sunday Best woollies.

- Meat was a once-a-week luxury. Food like suet pudding, vegetables and fish (which was surprisingly cheap) made up for the rest of the week.

- Many cottages had packed earth floors. Wooden floors were just stained and varnished and covered with home-made rag rugs.

- Piped water didn't arrive in the villages until the 1930's and even at that time, rural cottages were built with end-of-the-garden earth closets. In towns, houses still had outside loos but some of these had flushing cisterns! It was cold on a winter's night with only a candle to light your way!

- Our house was lit by gas until 1938. Mother's first fitted carpet was acquired in 1970 when she moved to Bracknell: her first carpet "square" had been positioned in 1940. Before the fitted carpet, we had loose rugs and polished lino, even acquiring several rolls of good quality lino from Clemerson's of Loughborough. Despite her protestations that it had been delivered in error, they never reclaimed it and so a good quality lino came to be fitted throughout out whole house!

- Cars for the ordinary man came well after the end of World War Two. If you managed to get your name down for a new car, you could, after a long wait for delivery, sell it on the black market for more than double the list price. Ford workers at Dagenham, for example, could pay £5 a month (a large sum at the time) into a club. Members took it in turn to get a £250 car. A three-bedroom semi in 1945 cost about £1000. The bungalow, with about 1/3 acre of land that we started to buy in 1950, cost £250 and when we sold it in 1962, it brought £4,500.

Violet Anne Denslow (19)

Fragment, Josie and Lenny

Italian sun beats down; our backs burn.
Man-child helping tame wild land.
Eyes swim; head aches; mirage teases me.
Is she real? Josie, this woman to be
My future to seal.

Rain gushes down foreign city gutters-
Like music to my ears .
No hiding from the sun behind closed shutters .

Familiar voices spin me round .
Through haze of smoke and laughter,
She stands before me, Josie, my happy-ever-after.

Lenny's Story

Accetura, where I was born in 1934, is situated in the instep of Italy's toe and is basically an agricultural area with a history dating from 1060. The beautiful Montepiano Woods, which are steeped in ancient traditions and social rites, cover large parts of this area and they were my youthful playground.

My parents, like most of the population, worked on the land, growing mostly cereal crops and while this might sound like an ideal existence, a beautiful pastoral setting, it should be remembered that the sun lives in southern Italy for a large part of the year. I recall one day when working in the searing heat with my father, both of us dehydrating by the second, that out of the heat mist appeared a vision, our neighbour's lovely little daughter Josie, and to quote my father, "Josie, if you go and fetch some water I'll let you marry my son Lenny."(I don't remember being allowed any opinion at this point.) The water father referred to came from a well over half an hour's walk away, so I guess I wasn't being sold cheap, and ever since our families have remained close friends.

Working on the land was seen as my natural future, following in father's footstep, but I found the temperature unbearable and longed for cooler climes with rain, so in 1960 when I was twenty six, I made my way to England. Nottingham had quite a large Italian community and my brother was already settled, so I joined him. With no knowledge of the English language, I had to work hard at learning from a dictionary, but because I had the determination, I succeeded and became very fluent. About six months after arrival in Nottingham, I was invited to an Italian wedding at St. Barnabas' Cathedral with a reception afterwards at a typical cheap-and-cheerful public house on Alfred Street. This turned out to be the happiest day of my life as I saw Josie again, now a very beautiful young woman. She was living with her brother. As far as I was concerned, it was love with a capital L and when we danced at the reception, I was in seventh heaven. My brother remarked that I was lucky to have met a girl from the same home town who was the right age. And he soon set about becoming my marriage broker.

The marriage was negotiated in Josie's sister's home and fortunately for me, Josie agreed to the proposal. After having considerably reduced my bank balance buying a ring at H. Samuel's, I did the expected thing and proposed on bended knee.

We had originally planned to marry in June but realised that if we made it before April 5th we would get all that year's tax back. This meant everything was rather a rush, having to find somewhere to live and getting bridal outfits, flowers and other such wedding paraphernalia. But it was worth it! Josie looked amazing and neither of us ever regretted it; in fact, in later years Josie often said, "After we die and go to heaven, I'll marry you again."

Our first home together was in a small terrace in Lichfield Road in Sneinton which we were able to buy as we were both working. I was employed by the Beeston Boiler Foundry making cast-iron radiators and Josie worked at a lace-manufacturers on Sherwood Rise. We lived happily in this little house for eight years and both our sons were born during this time, Anthony in 1963 and Giovanni in l966. In 1969 we were able to move into a bungalow in Maycroft Gardens off

Josie and Lenny's wedding day

Porchester Road which was very convenient for the schools that the boys attended, first the primary on Porchester Road, and then Manvers School.

By now I had changed my employers and was working for Boots and because I worked shifts, Josie and I were able to collect the boys from school and see that they had a secure home life. Much as we enjoyed our lives in Maycroft Gardens, when the opportunity to buy a house on Jarvis Avenue arose in 1979, we took it and have lived there ever since.

Josie was a child of nature and loved being outdoors in her garden, and this and her home was where she was happiest. She never longed for long holidays but just enjoyed the occasional days out visiting garden centres where she would find plants to enhance her beloved garden. Our house in Jarvis Avenue was one of the old farm properties and dated from the time when Bakersfield was an agricultural area. Naturally, with my upbringing, I knew how to treat the land well and consequently we grew more food than we could eat, so our neighbours benefited from home-grown runner beans, tomatoes, courgettes and cucumbers. Whilst Josie helped with the vegetables, her real interest was in flowers, and over the years she became an expert in taking cuttings and propagating them herself. As her favourite colour was yellow, the daffodils she grew were her pride and joy and in spring our garden was a riot of colour.

In 1970 we decided to try making our own wine. I had helped my parents when I was at home, so knew quite a bit about the rudimentary rules for making a good drink. I bought a press and a crusher and grapes by the pallet-load and spent many happy hours preparing the grapes for fermentation prior to bottling. We made enough wine, first in demijohns and then syphoned into bottles to last a year. If we had a good year I was able to put the odd bottle by so that I could establish a vintage cellar. It was hard work but worth it when one sat imbibing a glass of delicious home-made red wine in the evening sunlight. I completely agree with the doctor who said, "A glass of red wine a day does you the power of good."

Josie and I used to love cooking together and we would make enough tomato sauce from the fruit we grew in the garden to last us over half the year; we even used the bottles from our shop purchases earlier in the year. One thing I was never allowed to do was wash the dishes. I can't say that I found this a hardship !

In 1986 I began keeping fan-tailed doves, purchasing my first four birds from Melton Mowbray Cattle Market for £17 a pair on a Fur and Feathers Day. By the end of the first year, the birds had doubled in number, eventually reaching sixteen and I used to give the surplus away. Incidentally, prior to this, in the 1960s we visited the Nottingham Cattle

Market where we bought live chickens and if it was thought you had too many crushed into a box, a policeman would wring their necks!

In 1997, at the age of 63, I accepted a voluntary redundancy package from Boots where I had worked for thirty one years. This prevented a younger chap with a wife and children being made redundant. Although I retired two years early, I was no worse off and it gave me more time for my garden and birds. Josie at this time was working in the "rag trade" at the Marathon Works on Radford Boulevard but she took early retirement as well so that we could enjoy more time together.

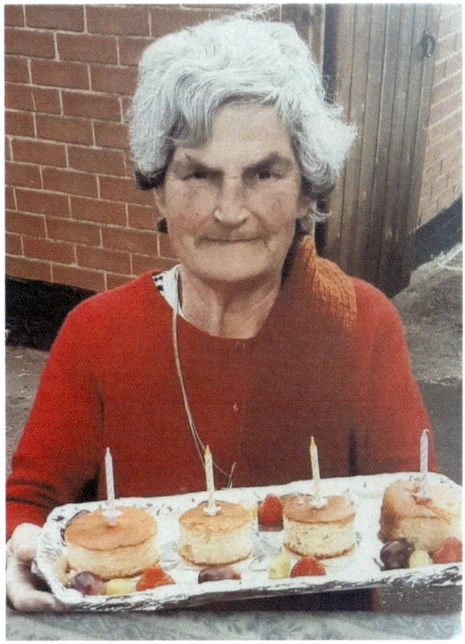
Josie's 80th birthday

Retirement meant we could spend more time visiting places like Rhyl, Llandudno, the sets of Coronation Street and Heartbeat, which were great favourites, as well as the Chelsea Flower Show. We once went to Jersey and stayed in St Hellier, but without doubt, our favourite place was Derbyshire with its lovely hills, river and valley scenery and the delightful towns of Matlock, Bakewell and our favourite, Ashbourne. But life was to change dramatically when Josie developed dementia.

Josie and Lenny at home

Dementia, Josie Scavetta

Dementia took Josie from me fifty-four years after we had married. It was slow and cruel, sucking out the person I knew till she was a husk of the strong, forthright, and very loving wife who had supported me throughout my life.

In the early stages, I just thought she wasn't listening to me, but the first concrete sign was she wasn't using the container for her false teeth which our son had bought, in fact, where were her teeth? Would you believe it, I discovered them tucked inside her bra, wrapped in tissue paper! She had taken to falling asleep on the sofa, removing her teeth as they hurt, folding them in tissue paper and pushing them inside her bra.

There was a dawning realisation that Josie was sick. We deny such things to ourselves, but there was no escaping the strange behaviour and lack of memory.

However, there were certain things which could not be erased from her memory, I could say, strong cultural traditions, learned young in Italy. These were about male/female roles – a woman's job and a man's job. I was allowed to prepare food and cook as I always had, but washing the dishes and cleaning up were out of bounds. In fact, if we were going about the chores when the doorbell rang, she'd send me to answer to make sure a friend or neighbour wouldn't see me doing "women's work"!!

Our problems were compounded by the fact that she knew she was ill but was too proud to tell even family. The pressure of secrecy weighed on me daily, and in my heart, I knew there was no sense in hiding her mental state. I felt it was in our best interests that family, friends and even strangers knew, so I tried to persuade her that she would be safer if she carried a card with her name and address. "What will you do if you take the bus to Arnold instead of Bakersfield and can't remember where you live!" I remonstrated, but logic knows no place in the mind of a person with dementia. It is also hard to understand how pride and embarrassment persist when the person can only remember the last word spoken, but these feelings were strong for Josie. I can hear her say, "What will people think of me? How can I let my husband do housework?" Yet those daily tasks have to be carried out, come what may, and in the end, Edwina, our devoted neighbour came to our rescue.

The grief and anguish I was feeling was unbearable at times. It lay heavily inside my chest, pressing down. How could I manage, knowing my wife was slowly being taken from me? Where was the woman I knew? Who was this person inside her body? I was crying as I walked round Tesco, feeling overwhelmed. But a familiar voice asked what was the matter. It was Edwina. Here was someone I could open up to. "She has dementia," I whispered. "I can help you," she reassured. Edwina had also noticed and she introduced me to the dementia support centre on Radford Road. I needed to be educated in coping with the woman I had known inside out as that woman was shrinking and a new person I didn't know, replacing her. I learned that I shouldn't show the anger or frustration I sometimes felt when she didn't respond, and I should not answer her questions if I felt unsettled but change the subject. Apparently, she may only remember the last word spoken and so could not answer lucidly. Patience and new strategies were things I had to learn quickly.

"I know Josie doesn't like you to clean but what the eye doesn't see, the heart doesn't grieve. Give me a key and I'll sneak in for two hours a day while you take Josie out." And so a pact was made with Edwina. It was the only way. Such practical help is necessary. At least we had a clean home, somewhere comfortable to rest and eat. I would take Josie out in the car and Edwina would let herself in to do all the domestic chores I wasn't allowed to do. And dear Edwina gave me the respite of getting to my allotment, a place of solace where I still grew the familiar potatoes, carrots, beetroot, French beans, Jerusalem artichokes and many more vegetables and fruit. How strange life is – here was abundant growth, life continuing as normal, side-by-side with that evil debilitating disease, dementia.

But such a pact with Edwina wasn't without its problems. On the days she cleaned, I knew we had to stay out two hours. Two hours can test the bladder of a normal person, let alone someone with dementia. When nature calls, it calls! Once, when she needed the loo, I pretended the car had broken down as the two hours weren't up. I reckoned the risk of Josie catching Edwina on her territory was worse than the risk of you know what!

Josie was very close to our son John, and without fail he rang her every night. In four years he missed only one night. This was a great solace to him and to her.

And so life continued with Josie, me, John and Edwina coping with dementia. Josie fought hard. An example of this was that she always fetched the daily paper for me. Duty again.

But dementia robbed her of the ability to read, so she didn't know which paper to buy. Ingeniously, as an aide-memoire, she cut the front page off a copy of The Daily Mail, kept it in her purse and tried to match it with the correct newspaper in the shop. One day, however, she returned to the shop three times and I got The Sun, The Star and The Daily Mail!

Josie and her son John

What she also didn't realise was that I, her Lenny, could no longer do everything for her. "Lenny will do it," was a common phrase. Not any more did I have the strength or the will. Also, dementia is selfish. She wanted the room warm, me, cool, so if I took off my socks and fell asleep, she would put them back on me and I'd wake up in a sweat. And in her desire to be a great housewife, she bought and hoarded vast quantities of cleaning products. Once, Edwina and I found a stash of twenty toothbrushes in their packaging, forty bars of soap, fifty-seven bottles of bleach and eighty-four packs of kitchen roll!

Josie's illness was compounded by two more events: the first, a fall down the stairs at home, and the second, by the pandemic of Covid-19.

The fall was in October 2020. The consequences were severe: she broke three bones in her pelvis and was hospitalised. I thought my heart would break. How could I stand more pain; how could she stand more suffering! Her mind was tortured and now she had broken bones and ulcerated legs. And when I thought we couldn't sustain any more blows, I too fell, aggravating an old back injury, and had to go into care for recuperation. This is a sad and anguished tale and my darling Josie had a stroke and had to return to hospital.

As I mentioned, by this time we were in the grip of Covid - effectively imprisoned, locked down, isolated. Josie ached to see us and we her, but all we could do was face-time her. The only way I manged this technology was with the painstaking help of our son John who meticulously drew and labelled diagrams of the mobile phone so I could successfully use face-time. But, how agonising it was to see her struggle to speak as the stroke had taken the use of her left side. Ironically, she called Covid "The Disease". Of course it was and is, but it was dementia that had stolen her true identity.

How dementia affects the brain I assume is well documented, but I believe doctors and carers are still learning. I tried to learn but you need all the support you can get. John and Edwina were my mainstays.

Death came on 4th February, 2021. We received "The Call" from the hospital, the one you don't want but the one you know is inevitable. My son John and I were blessed with forty-five minutes with her, her last. She squeezed our hands, knowing we were by her side, in particular, that I, Lenny, was there. She had suffered so much and couldn't understand why we weren't there every day. Covid kept us from her bedside. She wrote, "Perche non mi hai schiaffeggiato? Grazie per esserti preso cura di me!" "Why didn't you slap me, but thanks for looking after me."

John made the preparations for the funeral with an eye on appearances. "You can't go in Crocs or trainers, dad! " So he bought me four pairs of shoes to try and two suits and matching ties for us. We would be up to scratch. Also, in his true artistic style, he fashioned a photo built from old pieces of jewellery and added items depicting Josie's love of sewing – a needle, thimble, a button that looked like flowers, all put into a frame then sealed in a box with tape bearing world stamps to denote her connections to Italy. This momento would accompany his mum in her coffin. Whatsmore, the funeral was what she would have wanted. She was dressed in her best clothes and laid inside an exquisite open casket, and two fine horses decked in black plumes and sashes bearing her name, Guiseppina, drew the hearse to the church. The flowers were of course her favourite yellow, and my farewell was simply, "My Josie". I tell not a lie when I say the whole street came out to say their goodbyes, clapping solemnly as the horses drew her past them, along Jarvis Avenue to the top, and then to the Sacred Heart for mass.

The four years were so hard, so emotional, but now I'm left only with lingering memories, an empty house, and a lonely heart.

Fragment, Victor Britannica

I hug my secret to myself.
Only I will know when it is time to go .

My parents would be distraught, begging, " No! No!
Please, don't go."
With heart-breaking sobs, my name they will call.
I will slip away, like a cat in the night, shadowing a wall.

My little book I read alone, learning new words to help my plan:
" Work", "learn", "please", "thank you."

The time is right; my head is clear.
Me, two friends, just three young men stealing away
from loved ones held dear.

One: **single, the cardinal number**
Two: **the cardinal number that is the sum of one and one**.
That makes two of us.
Three: (a) **the cardinal number**;
(b) **pronoun, "Three were killed."**
The fear of what might lie ahead,
Through my body thrilled.

Victor's Story

This map may guide you through my journey, but as a fifteen-year old boy, I had no such map, and no map could help you travel the troubled tracks of my mind.

1990 was an inauspicious time to be born in the Middle East, but born I was. Saddam Hussein invaded his tiny but oil-rich neighbour, Kuwait, and the persecution of the Kurdish Iraqis began. Today, 30 million Kurds are stateless. I'm one of the lucky ones – I escaped to England and hold a solid British passport.

But that passport was only gained through a mixture of adolescent courage and bravado, together with the strength, dreams and the foolhardiness of youth.

Samar stroked my head and held me close to her slender

frame, her thick black hair falling over my shoulders. She was thirteen and I was five, and scared. Mama and papa had been forced to leave home to try and find work. We were penniless, robbed of our wealthy farmlands by the Iraqi government for being different, Kurdish. My eldest sister was my source of warmth, love and solace. " I will keep you safe," Samar promised, " but you will need to look after your younger brothers, at times." Hasan and Marwan were three and eighteen months, respectively. I could play football with them, but what else was I supposed to do? Sumeya, my other big sister, cooked and cleaned and smiled. Both Samar and Sumeya were so strong. Sumeya cooked us fluffy rice with delicious steaming turnips when she could. But, my favourite was Kalam-e-Malas, sweet and sour cabbage rolls, though we didn't have food every day. Best of all was when mama and papa could be with us, about once a fortnight. Then I felt safer.

Our close family-life was interrupted again when, at seven, I went to school. School was a distraction and I enjoyed learning to read and do basic calculations, arithmetic. But even at this early age, I knew life could be better. I wanted a mobile phone, Nike trainers and a Number 7 shirt to be like David Beckham. Actually, we barely had food, let alone luxuries: simple, meagre food and ragged clothes were the reality. In such circumstances, children grow up quickly, and at the age of eight, I started work after school, selling ice cream. It wasn't such a bad job; after all, it was the only time I got to lick the delicious sweet as it dribbled down my warm hands. How I smiled! I stuck at this job, and by the time I was ten, our financial situation was beginning to improve - some days we even had spicy kofte and kibbeh, cigar-shaped meat parcels, sweetened with cinnamon, a dish which my mother and sisters would ritualistically make together, chatting, singing and laughing. How we loved it.

Sadly, school was short-lived in our town, Kirkuk, and childhood, fleeting. At the age of twelve, I left school. It was 2002, and my real working life had begun. Like my father before me, I helped local farmers but I also bought and sold sweets at bus stops; I had the energy and the enterprise. In a matter of a couple of years, family life was looking better, more money coming in as papa rented out his old house and I had a number of different jobs which also brought in money.

What makes a young adolescent boy want to leave his family? The prospect of a better life I'd seen on TV, groups of boys playing football on a grass pitch, not a dirt street, music on demand, pizza, MacDonald's, motor bikes, Mercedes, high-rise flats and much more. Kirkuk is a 5,000 year-old city south of Erbil, the Kurdish capital, and bordered by the Hamrin mountains at a stunning height of 3,280 feet, a fact I was to learn later when I decided to leave at the age of fifteen.

We, me and two mates, Ibrahim, seventeen and Ahmed, eighteen, plotted and planned our escape from poverty and the cultural intolerance of the Iraqi State troopers. We met at night, squatting on street corners, sipping strong coffee and smoking harsh-tasting cigarettes. We were men and wouldn't hang around for whippings: we would forge a better future for ourselves. We knew we could do it. On the appointed day, we stuffed warm clothing, water and bread, a piece of goat's cheese and small slice of cured meat into our humble backpacks. Ahmed had been to the bus station and bought us three single tickets to Turkey. He shoved a fist full of grimy bank notes into the hand of the ticket attendant on the day of the Great Escape; she handed over the pristine tickets. How we smiled when he showed them to us, but he hung onto them as the "father" of the team. My contribution had been to teach myself a smattering of English from a tattered dictionary and Ibrahim said he was good at directions!

Turkey lay hundreds of miles over the mountains to the north west of Kirkuk, and was to be our first destination. Remember the map I've shared with you. The bus left at midnight, so I slipped out of the house around 10 p.m. My sisters and younger brothers were asleep but I couldn't resist a last look at Samar as she lay with Sumeya and the boys tucked up against her. I sighed and gently closed the door. But as I met the collaborators, a surge of adrenalin hit me. Here was the start of hope and adventure.

We needed to have our wits about us as we didn't have Turkish visas, so the plan was to weave and shift from one bus to another. As we pulled into the first dust-shrouded station high in the mountains, it was breaking dawn. Bleary-eyed travellers stumbled off the bus for a comfort-break. Indeed, comfort was needed after four hours on a bone-shaking bus on rough roads. We repeated this process several times, alert for guards and police who may stop our flight. We were already a band of brothers; we'd clasped hands in a sign of solidarity. We would make it! Travel-weary, we crossed the first milestone, the Turkish border, just as the sun was setting, then Istanbul! Golden! The great city straddling east and west, sitting on the magnificent Bosphorus. Such minarets and domes; cafes with sweets and pungent-smelling coffee and mint tea. But we needed to remain invisible and were fearful of the tough-looking police who would doubtless beat and imprison us if they caught us. Our night-time refuge was a bus stop with rough shelter of a concrete roof.

"My toes are frozen solid, " I dared to whisper.
" Get over yourself," Ahmed hissed. He was eighteen and tough. I was the baby, but I'd show them.
"And you look like a caveman with your beard!" I bandied.
"And you smell like an old goat," he hurled back.
Ibrahim smiled and nodded.

How thoughts turn into plans, how you seek out help or how help finds you is hard to say, but somehow, we found a man who would help us cross from Turkey to Greece. Well, money helps and at this stage we still had hard-earned cash! "I'm Kem," the small, grinning man offered. Thank goodness I'd learned a smattering of English. We must have looked in need of assistance. "Where you from, boys?" "Kurdistan!" I answered, puffing my small chest up with pride. "So, you'll be need van. Need go Greece. I help you." Money was handed over and we were optimistic. Foolish! The van arrived and we squashed in with fifteen other young hopeful men. Three hours on the unmade road left us shaking. The driver stopped the van abruptly, "Everyone out here!" he shouted. "But, where are we?" someone dared. "Don't be brave," a voice suggested, and then I heard it for the first time, "People-traffickers!" I understood. We were being shoved forwards and unsure what our destination would be and what might happen in the hands of ruthless smugglers. We were to be smuggled into Greece. "Walk," said someone. He appeared to be in charge. "You walk three hours. You be fine." What else could we do? We didn't know where we were, there was no shelter and the air, chilling. We walked, not three but six hours. Those border lands are treacherous, scrubby, rocky, with wild animals, thieves, so we stuck together, almost like a chain gang. " Come on, guys," said Ahmed. "We're tough Kurds. We can do it!" As darkness fell, we arrived by a river, the mighty river Marilsa, 300 miles long. It acts as a natural barrier between Turkey and Greece, a route for migrants, flowing into the mythical Aegean.

The small boat bobbed up and down. "Get in," we were ordered, and of course, we obeyed. "Not much choice," I thought, tugging my hoodie further over my forehead and tightly clinging to my rucksack with its few worldly goods - a small comfort. Could this tiny boat even carry us safely? "Move up," snapped someone. So we huddled up to strange men who spoke many different languages but had one purpose, and so we allowed ourselves to be ferried we knew not where.

The "where" was a small Greek island. As we fell out of the boat into the warm water, I was happy to have survived and to wash away some of the filth that had attached to my body on the journey thus far. But, mosquitoes feasted on us and we couldn't take the rest we needed. The locals were friendly, thankfully, but we still had to buy food from them. After that, the facts have become muddled in my head. I know we had to cross another river and on the other side we were swallowed by forest and mountains from whence we trudged for a further twelve to fourteen hours. I don't know how I put one foot in front of the other. Blood dripped from my gashed feet and thoughts of death were never too far away. "Come on, brother. You can make it," panted

Ahmed. It was as much as I could do to nod. We had no choice but to keep moving. "Keep walking," commanded the smugglers, who beat us if we faltered. "You can soon rest and eat. There will be water too."

Night came and went and dawn brought nothing, no food, no water, just more pain. My stomach ached for food and I imagined eating kibbeh and rice, washed down with a large glass of cool spring water. I suddenly longed for my home, for my parents, for Samar. "Ibrahim, what direction are we heading in?" I asked, as if that mattered. "Due west. Can't you see the sun!"

Fatigue and hunger blur the mind, so all I can say is some time later, a large lorry arrived and we were loaded like cattle, squashing up against many others who were already on board. There must have been about fifty of us, packed into a secret compartment within a container to evade detection.

"I can't breathe, Ahmed," I whispered. "We're going to die here, like sheep."
"We have come this far. We will make it. Breathe slowly, and shut up."
Ibrahim nodded.

I think I must have passed out or slept but Ahmed and Ibrahim said ten hours had passed and we had arrived in Athens. I woke to the stench of sweat, and worse, defecation.

We had been broken up into groups, and we three were joined by another twelve. We groggily disembarked, our bodies weak and shaky and we were taken to a private house where we had to hand over more money. Ahmed, Ibrahim and I clung together but our ordeal wasn't yet over. Many more miles and hardships were to follow. To start with, we were hungry like we'd never been before or since, but worse than that, were the "jackals" who snapped at our heels and pushed us ever forwards, many times into danger. We were commodities, not humans.

At this point in the journey, we were once again alone, abandoned, with no knowledge of the language and very little money. But just as despair sets in, there can be a blessed moment of hope. Miraculously, Ahmed found a friend of his working in a coffee shop. Breathlessly, he cried, "Victor, Ibrahim, come. God is good. He has led us to my friend. He can help us!"

Oh, how I cried. Tears of joy and disbelief smudged the dirt on my face. For the first time in weeks, we stayed in a clean flat and ate food. After a good night's sleep, he took us to an area where there were Kurdish restaurants and shops. I was even able to call my family.

"Oh my God! Victor, where are you? We thought you were dead. Come home. We love you. Your sisters are so sad without you. How can we manage? Come home, our son!" my mother begged.

" I have come this far, to Greece. We are nearly at the end of our journey. I can't give up and I will see you again one day. I love you."

I called mum again the following day and she agreed to send £100, a lot of money for her, and I hoped it would see me through to the end of my journey.

We had travelled over 3,000 miles to Greece and yet our journey was not finished. "Greece is poor. You would be better off in England where people are more open-minded," persuaded an Iranian Kurd. "I can help you to get a passport and flights to France. From there, it will be easy to get into the U.K."

The little English I knew spurred me on to make a last effort to find a better life. As the plane landed at Charles de Gaulle airport, my friends and I were excited. Not long now, we thought, but once again we were tricked and the taxi driver who picked us up took us to The Britannia Hotel in a seedy suburb of Paris, not Britain as I had understood. How could people be so cruel? We were young and helpless and yet the taxi driver robbed me of all the money I had. I fell asleep on a park bench and awoke to the sound of church bells.

Britain was still a million miles away, but I had come this far, suffered this much. I would survive. Survive, I did, and Nottingham, here I am. But what became of Ahmed and Ibrahim I do not know. I hope they are well. God bless us all.